M&GN in Colour

VOLUME I

Edited by Dennis Greeno

Midland and Great Northern Joint Railway Society
Sheringham Station
Sheringham
Norfolk

The M&GN were joint owners with the Great Eastern Railway of the line from Yarmouth to Lowestoft, the construction of which was undertaken by the GE, with the M&GN providing their own connection from Yarmouth Beach over Breydon Bridge. Titled the 'Norfolk & Suffolk Joint Railway', it is considered part of the M&GN for the purposes of this publication.

First published 2009
Reprinted with corrections 2012

© The Midland and Great Northern Joint Railway Society

ISBN 978-0-904062-50-2

The Midland and Great Northern Joint Railway Society,
Sheringham Station
Sheringham
Norfolk NR26 8RA

Design, photograph preparation and typeset by Dennis Greeno MCSD
The only costs incurred by the publisher were for copyright fees, printing and binding.

Printed in England

TEXT AND CAPTIONS WRITTEN BY RICHARD ADDERSON, STEVE ALLEN AND DOUG WATTS

Acknowledgements

During the course of obtaining a photograph for use in *Joint Line* I came into contact with Colour-Rail for the first time and its owner Ron White. A four word scribble by him on a compliments slip, 'there's more, just ask' started off a process that has culminated in this booklet, the first of a series of four. As the project has progressed other colour material has come to light but the vast majority of photographs are from the Colour-Rail library.

I do not have the knowledge to write with any authority on the M&GN so I was grateful for the help offered by Richard Adderson, Steve Allen and Doug Watts. Mick Clark, president of the M&GN Circle, has checked the proofs whilst Adrian Vaughan has assisted with details on signalling. Mike Back and Robert Powell subsequently offered some suggestions after the volume was first published that have been incorporated into this reprint. My thanks go to all seven – photographs may say a thousand words but in my experience they can be immeasurably enhanced when coupled with authoritative writing.

If you would like to know more about the fascinating history of the M&GN, the M&GN Circle was formed in 1959 for those interested in the railway. For details send a self stamped addressed envelope to Graham Kenworthy, 16 Beverley Road, Brundall, Norwich NR13 5QS.

And, of course, thanks to Ron White without whom you would not be reading this now.

Sources

Clark M J 1990 *Midland and Great Northern Joint Railway*, Ian Allan (Railway World Special)
Digby N, *A Guide to the Midland and Great Northern Joint Railway*, Ian Allan, 1993
Rhodes J, *The Midland & Great Northern Joint Railway*, Ian Allan, 1982
Wilkinson E, *Operation Norfolk*, Xpress Publishing, 2008
Wrottesley A J, *The Midland & Great Northern Joint Railway*, David & Charles, 1970
The District Controller's View: No. 12 The Midland and Great Northern Joint Railway, Xpress Publishing, 2009
M&GN Circle *Bulletin*
M&GNJRS *Joint Line*

THE LATE H N JAMES/COLOUR-RAIL/LM19

Saxby was where through trains bound for the M&GN left the Midland Railway's Leicester to Peterborough line. Here we see a through Birmingham to Great Yarmouth train at Saxby headed by LMS 2P class 542, and Midland 4F class 4032. The famous 'Leicesters', the daily through workings, were usually hauled throughout by M&GN engines – the fact this has LMS motive power indicates that it may have been an excursion. In the 1930s when LMS locomotives worked trains bound for the M&GN they were usually changed here at Saxby or Bourne. In the 1940s and 1950s this changeover took place at South Lynn. It is unclear, in this August 1936 photograph, whether the 2P pilot engine is being added or whether both locomotives are being detached. The 2Ps were still to be seen on the western section during the 1950s, but the 4Fs were more common visitors, taking trains to South Lynn, Melton, and sometimes right through to Great Yarmouth. Prior to the 1936 LNER takeover, two 4Fs, nos. 3913 and 4265 were on loan from the LMS and stationed at South Lynn.

This well-known image is the only known colour photograph of a M&GN-liveried locomotive. Taken at Edmondthorpe and Wymondham in 1936, it shows M&GN DA class 0-6-0 89 and an unidentified LMS 4F. Although hard to believe, the livery under the grime is actually M&GN chocolate brown. Note the raised brass numerals on the cabside. At this date the M&GN only had a few months remaining before coming under LNER auspices on 1 October 1936. Eighty-six were manufactured in Glasgow by Dübs and Co. in 1900 to a Great Northern Railway design produced by H A Ivatt. As with many M&GN engines it acquired aspects of both owning companies and here it is sporting a Midland-style Deeley smokebox door, though oddly offset from the centre of the smokebox. It was renumbered as LNER 089 in April 1937, later to become 4164 in the 1946 LNER renumbering scheme. The locomotive was scrapped in 1947. Edmondthorpe and Wymondham was not on the M&GN proper, being the first station east of Saxby on the Midland Railway line that met the M&GN end-on at Little Bytham junction.

Express services in the 1930s

By the end of the first decade of the twentieth century the M&GN had two regular express services that ran every day of the week, except Sunday, throughout the year. These were a train from King's Cross to Cromer *via* Peterborough and South Lynn and one from Birmingham to Yarmouth *via* Saxby and South Lynn. The latter became known as the 'Leicester' as it passed through that city on its way from Birmingham. These express services continued to run through the summer months when they were supplemented on Saturdays by express trains for holidaymakers. Unlike resorts such as Blackpool, that attracted a large number of day trippers, the distance between Norfolk and industrial Britain meant the M&GN specialised in carrying holidaymakers planning a week or a fortnight stay on the coast. After its formation in 1893 the M&GN encouraged the growth of these summer Saturday services, a pattern continued by the LMS and later the LNER.

Whereas Yarmouth and Cromer were already established resorts, the Sheringham area was very much the creation of the railways. The population rose from around 1,250 in 1881 to just over 4,500 in 1931. By the late 1930s significant numbers of summer Saturday expresses were running from the Midlands to these three destinations. In the last summers before the outbreak of World War II the basic timetable of trains from the Midlands to Yarmouth on a summer Saturday consisted of the regular daily Birmingham–Yarmouth service plus trains from Manchester, Nottingham and Derby and extra services from Birmingham and Leicester. On a summer Saturday, Cromer enjoyed its own services from Leicester, Birmingham and Manchester as well as the regular service from King's Cross. These services would have been supplemented by a number of special workings to or from the coast.

THE LATE H N JAMES/COLOUR-RAIL/NE45

In the immediate period after the M&GN had been absorbed by the LNER and many of its locomotives had been withdrawn, the LNER cascaded many older pre-grouping 4-4-0s to the M&GN. In 1937, 12 ex-Great Central D9 class 4-4-0s were allocated to the M&GN section to work the heavier trains. In this June 1946 photograph, 6018 works hard up Edmondthorpe bank with a Birmingham–Yarmouth M&GN service composed of Midland and LMS coaches. By this time, 6018 was one of only four of the class remaining on the M&GN and by the following March they had all been withdrawn or re-allocated elsewhere. The filthy condition and the badly burned smokebox door are indicative of the run-down state of the locomotives in the immediate post war period, but mechanically it appears in very good condition.

RAY REED/COLOUR-RAIL

Ivatt 4MT class 43085 on an east-bound train at Bourne on the last day of most passenger services on the M&GN, 28 February 1959. The locomotive was allocated to Peterborough New England shed during its M&GN career. Bourne was the first station on the M&GN west of Little Bytham junction. It was at Bourne that the M&GN met and crossed the Great Northern lines from Essendine and Sleaford. Bourne was a substantial station with large goods shed and engine shed – the water tower for the shed can be seen behind the engine. Unusually, the main station building was a seventeenth century merchantman's home of the Stuart period that was purchased by the Bourne and Essendine Railway in 1857. It was used as a ticket office only until 1893, when the station was rebuilt. although it remained in other forms of railway use until closure. After 1893, tickets were issued from an office forming part of the island platform buildings. The merchantman's house has subsequently been fully restored and is now a civic amenity for the town.

The Ivatt 4MTS

By the early 1950s the M&GN section was a part of British Railways Eastern Region. The rag-bag locomotives inherited from the LNER in the pre-war years to replace the ageing M&GN locomotives were themselves becoming life expired.

In a bold move to rejuvenate M&GN services the British Transport Commission agreed in 1950 to the allocation of 50 brand new H G Ivatt-designed 4MT class 2-6-0s. The first of these engines had been produced in the last month of the LMS as a modern replacement for pre-grouping 4-4-0s, and although functional and ugly, they were more than adequate for the M&GN services. They became synonymous with the M&GN in BR days and remained on the system to the end.

A total of 162 of these locomotives were built and fortunately one of the class still exists. 43106 was based on the M&GN at South Lynn depot when new in April 1951 until June 1956 and is preserved at the Severn Valley Railway at Bridgnorth in Shropshire.

Melton-based 43147 is seen heading east at Aylsham North in 1958. Aylsham was a busy crossing loop, being able to accommodate the longest of trains. Such were their number through on a summer Saturday that the signalman would be provided with an assistant to collect the single line tablets. Note the lineside Whitaker tablet exchange apparatus just in front of the locomotive. The filthy, leading coach is a LMS (period III) Stanier full brake in unlined BR maroon livery.

THE LATE E ALGER/COLOUR-RAIL

The beautifully kept state of this idyllic country station at Stalham in September 1958 belies the fact it was to close just five months later on 28 February 1959. This photograph shows well the mixed origins of the railway infrastructure. On the Down platform, the station building was a contractor design, being erected by Wilkinson and Jarvis in 1880. The coach body next to it is an old Eastern and Midlands Railway vehicle used as a goods office. Just off the Up platform is a typical M&GN concrete block permanent way hut, whilst a little way along is an Eastern and Midlands lift-type water crane. Further up is a wooden waiting shelter and then a Midland-style signal box. After closure Stalham station and yard became a Norfolk County Council Highways Department depot. The A149 Stalham bypass took the route of the line just to the east of the station. In 2000 the County Council offered the station building to the North Norfolk Railway – it was removed brick by brick and painstakingly rebuilt at its Holt station. After 45 years of dereliction, the building hosted its first passenger train on 28 February 2004.

On 16 August 1958, J17 class 65586 of Yarmouth Beach pulls away from Potter Heigham heading a 'Holiday Camps Express' on the final stage of its journey from Liverpool Street to Caister on Sea. By the 1950s this was the only through service from south-east England to the M&GN. The train joined the M&GN at North Walsham where there was a connection with the Great Eastern Norwich to Cromer line. This class of locomotive was designed for freight duties and could be seen on goods trains throughout East Anglia, but some were fitted with vacuum brakes for passenger working from 1942 onwards . It is probable the locomotive is running tender first as it had brought the London-bound 'Holiday Camps Express' into North Walsham and there were no facilities at North Walsham to turn it before returning in the Yarmouth direction with the service from London. This was the only summer Saturday service, other than the regular Birmingham–Yarmouth service, to offer what would be called today 'on-train catering'. The public timetable noted, 'light refreshments available'. In all probability, this was nothing more than a trolley as no buffet car was scheduled for this train.

More typical of the M&GN were the services from and to the Midlands. On 20 July 1957, the 8.19 am from Yarmouth Beach to Chesterfield is heading north behind B12/3 61530. The location is California Cliff close to where the line leaves the coast and heads west to Great Ormesby. For most of the 1950s at least two B12s were allocated to Yarmouth, mainly for the Midland expresses. These 4-6-0s tended to take out the heavier trains in the summer. This summer (Saturday only) service to Nottingham and Chesterfield from Yarmouth followed an unusual route on the M&GN. Most trains travelled *via* Bourne (*see* map), but this train headed to Peterborough by way of Sutton Bridge and Wisbech. On reaching Peterborough it halted on the former Midland lines to the west of the station, and another engine backed on to the other end of the train which then ran north by way of Stamford to Nottingham. This manoeuvre was presumably to reduce pressure on the predominantly single line from Sutton Bridge.

In this second photograph of a Midlands-bound service, holidaymakers enjoy a final view of the sea from the dunes, south of Caister on Sea, as the last summer express of the day, the 3.00 pm Yarmouth to Leicester behind 43142, makes its way home in mid afternoon on 10 August 1957. The six coaches on this train will be joined by another four or five from Cromer at Melton Constable before continuing west. With a combined load of 11 carriages it was one of the heavier trains of the day. It arrived back in Leicester at 8.10 pm – a journey time of over five hours. The train is unusual in two ways. First, it was the only summer Saturday train to leave Yarmouth after midday. Secondly, because it left in the afternoon, it was one of only two summer expresses where the carriages that had arrived earlier in the day were used on the return service. These coaches had arrived at Yarmouth in the morning as the 9.00 am from Leicester. Most stock was stored either in Yarmouth or the Midlands in between the Saturday workings.

Summer expresses in the 1950s

After the war the summer Saturday seaside expresses returned to the M&GN as did the regular Birmingham–Yarmouth service. However, the King's Cross to Cromer train was not reinstated and the summer Saturday trains from Manchester were discontinued. Holidaymakers now came almost exclusively from the east or west Midlands, and especially Nottingham, Derby and Leicester. In the summer timetables of the 1950s, Monday to Friday services varied little from those of the winter months, but summer Saturdays were very different. The M&GN continued its tradition of bringing holidaymakers from industrial Britain to the east and north coasts of Norfolk – and the northern Suffolk coast until 1953. Day excursion traffic on the M&GN main line was unusual, although in the west it fed daytripper traffic into the Great Eastern resort of Hunstanton. As in the 1930s, from the point of view of the M&GN, Sheringham, Cromer and Yarmouth were predominantly one and two week holiday destinations. A good example of these services is provided by the busiest Saturday of the final summer in 1958 when 18 expresses ran between South Lynn and Melton Constable on their way from the Midlands to the coast. On this Saturday, as in the 1930s, Yarmouth was the main destination with 4,500 seats provided, with 800 to Sheringham and Cromer. The 18 expresses included a regular summer Friday/Saturday overnight service departing from Shirebrook, north of Nottingham, and two additional overnight services – from Congleton and Nuneaton. Summer Saturday expresses to the coast averaged around eight coaches in length offering over 300 seats per train. One Saturday, in late July 1958, just over 3,200 tickets were collected from passengers who had arrived at Yarmouth from stations west of Peterborough – the equivalent of between 60 and 70 modern 50-seater coaches.

B1 class 4-6-0 61233 crosses the road bridge just south of Hopton station with a nine-coach 'Holiday Camp Express' from Liverpool Street on 14 June 1958. Hopton station stood on an embankment and Mr Alger, the photographer, was looking along the sloping driveway leading to the platforms from road level. Partly obscured by the gatepost, one of the village children is pushing a barrow towards the station in the hope of earning a few coppers for helping passengers with their luggage.

The train we saw in the previous photograph has now come to a stand in the platform at Hopton station. A number of local youngsters are waiting with their barrows by the station exit, ready to supplement their pocket money by helping the holidaymakers transport their cases to the holiday camp, which was nearly a mile away. To the left of the picture, a young lady has already struck a deal with two of the alighting passengers, and two cases are loaded on her home-made trolley. The signal beyond the train is at danger, indicating that Hopton signal box was in use that day – it was not normally used at quieter times.

It is the end of the holiday. In a scene reminiscent of a suburban rush hour, passengers throng the platform at Hopton on the sunny morning of Saturday 24 August 1958, waiting to board the train that will take them back to London and the reality of the working week. Everything seems to be unhurried – people were accustomed to taking their turn in the queue in those days. It is likely that specific coaches were allocated to passengers from each station, which would have evened out the loading of the train. The lady with long hair in the centre foreground is carrying a crash helmet – does that suggest there is a scooter stored somewhere on the train? At the platform end a tender-first J15 simmers away, but it will be a few minutes before everyone is aboard and the train is ready to depart.

GORLESTON
Super
HOLIDAY CAMP

SUPER to the last detail
Ideally situated in secluded private grounds three minutes from sea and within easy reach of shops, theatres, etc.
All chalets and bedrooms have hot and cold water, some with bath and toilet, and are serviced daily.
Spacious and luxurious Dining Room, Ballroom, Lounges, Bar and Games Rooms.
Magnificent Swimming Pool. Superb food prepared by highly experienced Chefs and served by Waiters.
Free colour brochure from

Gorleston-on-Sea Holiday Camp Ltd.
Great Yarmouth, Norfolk.
Member N.F.P.H.C.   Phone : Gorleston 1721

Judging by the length of the shadows, it is quite early in the day as an unidentified D16/3 heads an Up train towards Bridge Road, just south of Gorleston station, on Saturday, 2 August 1958. The timetable would suggest that the train is the 8 am from Gorleston, which will call at Hopton, Corton, Lowestoft and then most stations on the East Suffolk line to Ipswich, before running non-stop to Liverpool Street. Arrival in the capital was scheduled for 11.31 am. The scene is still recognisable today, although the trackside gardens are now overgrown and back on to a footpath that follows the route of the railway hereabouts.

The holiday camp, in the background, was proud of its 'ideal' location in secluded private grounds which was used to great effect in its advertising. However, the adjacent railway line was not mentioned even to the extent that it was air-brushed out of the aerial photograph.

The Great Eastern Railway 4-4-0s

It was an irony that after the M&GN's own locomotives had been sent for scrapping at Stratford, in the east of London, after the 1936 LNER takeover, many engines from its former 'enemy' the Great Eastern Railway should be drafted in to take their places. However, the M&GN enginemen were quick to realise their potential. LNER D15 class 'Claud Hamiltons', designed by James Holden of the GER at the end of the nineteenth century, started to arrive early in 1939 and were put to use across the system.

By the mid-1940s they were supplemented by some of the newer Gresley rebuilds, the D16/3s. At least 50 ex-GER 4-4-0s are recorded as having worked on the M&GN at some point in time. Whilst popular engines, they proved to be underpowered for the 'Leicesters' and so a handful of B12/3s were transferred in for these services in 1948. The D16/3s remained on the line until the closure.

It is unfortunate that none of these stylish engines survived into preservation but as the last of the class was withdrawn in 1960, before railway preservation got off the ground, it is not surprising.

THE LATE E ALGER/COLOUR-RAIL

D16/3 class 4-4-0 62604 runs into Corton with an Up train on 8 June 1957. The roofboard on the second coach indicates this is one of the 'Holiday Camp Express' trains that ran between Gorleston and Liverpool Street on summer Saturdays to cater for the booming holiday industry. 62604 is running over the points giving access to the goods yard. The engine was allocated to Yarmouth Southtown locomotive shed at the time and would therefore have been a regular visitor to the line. On arrival at Lowestoft Central, the train would reverse, and a main line locomotive, possibly a B1 or 'Sandringham' take over for the onward journey to London *via* the East Suffolk line and Ipswich. The train is passing the Up home signal and the Down advance starter can be seen on the left of the photograph.

BRIAN SULLIVAN COLLECTION

Peterborough North was the south-west outpost of the M&GN. On 31 January 1959 Ivatt 43144, a South Lynn-shedded locomotive during its eight years on the M&GN, sits at the station in the early afternoon at the head of a train for Great Yarmouth. Peterborough North was shared with the Midland, Great Northern and latterly, with the closure of Peterborough East, Great Eastern services from the town. The M&GN services usually started from the Down bay platform at the north end of the station. On leaving the station they followed the GN Down main until turning left at Westwood Junction (to reach the Midland lines) and then quickly left again at Wisbech Junction to reach the M&GN proper. From Wisbech Junction M&GN trains proceeded to climb up and over the route to the north on New England Bridge no. 1, known locally as 'Rhubarb Bridge', before heading east across the Fens. The leading coach would appear to be a standard LNER Gresley compartment brake third in lined maroon livery. Peterborough North is long since gone, the current station was built on the site, and the Up fast now follows the route of the Arcade siding situated to the left of 43144.

Large structures on the M&GN

Although most of the M&GN was built across flatlands the terrain did not prevent the M&GN from having a handful of substantial structures. From west to east, the first was on the approaches to Bourne, the five-arch Lound Viaduct which was followed closely by the 330 yards (297 metres) Toft Tunnel – the only tunnel on the M&GN. Next came Cross Keys Bridge at Sutton Bridge over the river Nene and on the approach to South Lynn was the M&GN's five-span West Lynn Bridge over the Great Ouse. East of Lynn major structures were avoided until the line reached the Broads and crossed the river Thurne at Potter Heigham on a three-span girder bridge. On the Cromer branch there were parallel viaducts at East Runton carrying the M&GN towards Cromer, and the Norfolk and Suffolk to Mundesley. By far the largest, and most impressive, structure was Breydon Bridge – one of its five spans was a swing bridge – across Breydon Water at Great Yarmouth linking the M&GN at Yarmouth Beach with the Norfolk and Suffolk Joint at North Gorleston Junction. Opened in 1903, the bridge was closed in 1953 and demolished nine years later.

COLOUR-RAIL

Cross Keys Bridge was, and still is, the gateway into Norfolk for many travellers from the Midlands, north and north-west. This is a view of it from the station footbridge on the west side of the river on the last day of services. South Lynn's 43111 is running light through the station, possibly working its way off the M&GN to a new home. The Midland Railway-designed signal boxes, with distinctive hipped roofs, at each side of the bridge can be clearly seen.

COLOUR-RAIL

In the last summer of operation on the M&GN we see 43109 – another South Lynn resident – crossing the swing bridge heading for South Lynn on 23 August 1958. In this photograph the solid construction of the bridge is evident, as is the operating 'bridge' in the octagonal turret. The train is formed of ex-LNER Gresley standard corridor stock in a mixture of carmine and cream and maroon liveries.

Cross Keys Bridge at Sutton Bridge

The river Nene at Sutton Bridge is a natural boundary between the Norfolk and Lincolnshire – though the actual county boundary does not match it exactly. Until the 17th century this area was salt marshes, and over the subsequent 200 years the land was gradually reclaimed. It was not until 1828 when the Nene was embanked to drain the marshes that the first bridge was built to open up a direct route from King's Lynn to Newark avoiding the need to travel *via* Wisbech. In 1850 the early bridge was replaced with a swing bridge designed by Robert Stephenson. This was initially a road bridge, but with the building of the line from South Lynn in 1866, the railway had parliamentary powers to use it for rail traffic on a shared deck. By 1892 this second structure was insufficient for the growing levels of traffic, so the M&GN built the current Cross Keys Bridge to the south of, and adjacent to, the earlier bridge. Although the M&GN would have preferred a rail only bridge (retaining the previous bridge for road traffic)it was built with dedicated, adjacent rail/road thoroughfares to meet objections from the river authorities who would not allow two bridges in such close proximity. Until 1903 a road toll was charged for crossing. The bridge was originally hydraulically worked with its movements being controlled from the octagonal turret on top of it.

Since the line closed in 1959, the rail side of the bridge has been converted to carry west-bound road traffic, partially easing the bottleneck of a single width road crossing. As part of the main A17 route into Norfolk the bridge is still an important gateway into the county, and plans for a replacement came to nothing with the Highways Agency opting to strengthen and increase the headroom on the old bridge. This relic of the M&GN will be with us for many more years as a reminder of when the line crossed the Fens and the river Nene.

COLOUR-RAIL

A photograph taken from the octagonal bridge control room on the final day, ex-GNR J6 class 64172, which was based at Peterborough New England, approaches with a west-bound freight, having just come along the causeway adjacent to the A17 which runs on the bank in the background. The fireman has taken the single line token from the signalman after leaving the double track section from South Lynn. The green Ford Anglia 100E on the A17 has the road almost to itself, a situation that was to change dramatically in the following decade with increased congestion, even with the rail side converted to road. These days the realigned A17 has obliterated all traces of the railway between West Lynn Bridge and Cross Keys Bridge.

The same train as in the previous photograph is seen entering Sutton Bridge station. In the foreground is the splendid M&GN concrete junction signal with somersault arms. To the left is the goods shed that stood at a right angle to the 1897 bridge as it was aligned with the earlier 1850 bridge that was located further north. The left hand somersault is in the 'off' position indicating the train was entering the goods loop thus avoiding the platform lines. It was due to the siting of the current bridge that Sutton Bridge station was built on a sharp curve.

Melton Constable was the hub of the M&GN with lines radiating to Norwich in the south, South Lynn and beyond to the west, Great Yarmouth to the east, and Cromer to the north. The 15 mile line to Cromer had started as an attempt by the Eastern and Midlands Railway to reach the north coast port of Blakeney in the 1880s. Having run out of money when they had covered the five miles to Holt the directors decided that Cromer, then a popular seaside resort with the adjacent 'Poppyland', would be a more viable proposition. Thus the line was built from Holt to Cromer, most of which survives today. In this photograph of August 1958, we see former Great Eastern D16/3 class 62597 leaving Melton Constable at Melton West junction and taking the Cromer line. 62597 was a Melton Constable locomotive at this time and local workings such as these on the Cromer and Norwich branches would have been its main duties. The leading coach is an LNER pre-war steel panelled vehicle, painted in early 1950s carmine as applied to non-corridor and parcels vehicles between 1950 and 1956.

A fine portrait of Ivatt 4MT class 43147 standing next to the coaling stage at Cromer Beach in September 1957. 43147 was allocated new to the M&GN in late 1951 and was shedded at Melton Constable during its eight years on the Joint, moving to Boston in 1959. It was withdrawn in January 1966.

These days it is difficult to imagine the enthusiasm with which the new diesel multiple units were greeted when they burst on to the railway scene in the 1950s. Generally they were clean, light and spacious, particularly when compared with the ageing steam-hauled coaches they replaced, and the front seats, giving a view of the driver's activity and the track ahead, were much sought after. Encapsulating the new image, a smart green Derby lightweight diesel unit leaves Corton on a local working from Yarmouth Southtown to Lowestoft on 17 April 1958. The large building above the rear coach is the house provided for the station master. Passenger services survived longer on the N&SJ than the M&GN. The Yarmouth Southtown to Lowestoft route closed in May 1970.

Diesels on the M&GN

Despite the rapid switch to diesel traction in East Anglia during the late 1950s, the M&GN main line was operated almost exclusively by steam locomotives right up to the time it closed in 1959, although in the late 1950s small diesel shunters could be found working at larger stations such as Melton Constable, Yarmouth Beach and South Lynn. In addition, most trains on the Norwich and Cromer branches were operated by diesel multiple units from September 1957 onwards.

The former Norfolk and Suffolk line between Yarmouth and Lowestoft had become very much part of the main line Great Eastern system after it had become isolated from the M&GN system following the closure of the line over Breydon Bridge in 1953. As part of the GE system it was operated by engines from former GER sheds, and was regularly visited by diesel locomotives, mainly the numerous Brush Type 2s, as well as diesel multiple units on more local services.

With the rapid abolition of steam traction the sections of the remaining M&GN system, which were retained for freight, inevitably became diesel worked in their final years.

THE LATE E ALGER/COLOUR-RAIL

Brush Type 2 D5565 curves past Corton's Up distant signal with a passenger train on 17 April 1961. At this time 27 Up and 26 Down trains were timetabled over the line each weekday, an intensity of service which had only been rivalled on summer Saturdays in years gone by. This was the result of the closure of the direct line between Yarmouth and Beccles in November 1959, which meant that all trains to and from Yarmouth Southtown were routed *via* the former N&S Joint line. Towards the end of the 1960s British Railways adopted the Total Operations Processing System (TOPS) so these Type 2 diesels became 'Class 31' and as a result D5565 was renumbered 31147. It was withdrawn in September 1996 and cut up in April 2001.

ROB TIBBITTS/COLOUR-RAIL

Whilst many sections of the M&GN were ripped up with undue haste after the February 1959 closure (some said, by a BR management intent on ensuring that the line could not be preserved or reopened), some sections remained open for freight into the mid-1960s and beyond. One such stretch was the route from Spalding to Sutton Bridge that lasted until 1 May 1965. Here filthy Ivatt 4MT 43068 runs tender first from Spalding through Gedney with a solitary LMS-designed brake van to pick up the afternoon Class C parcels service from Long Sutton (*see* panel). The locomotive was originally a Peterborough, then a South Lynn-based engine, but was transferred away to Boston after the closure. When this photograph was taken, on 3 September 1963, much of the freight on the remains of the M&GN was diesel hauled but some steam hauled services lasted on this section until at least November 1964. Gedney station was still in a neat and tidy condition even though four years have elapsed since its closure to passengers.

End of freight on the western section

On the lines west of South Lynn the surviving freight services depended upon a variety of customers whereas, in the eastern section, freight's survival depended mainly on the existence of a few large clients. The western section freight lines radiated from either Spalding, to Sutton Bridge and Bourne, or Murrow where two short sections of line ran west to Dogsthorpe and east to Wisbech. Formerly, the M&GN crossed over the Great Northern and Great Eastern line from March to the north on the level with no rail connection but, after closure of the M&GN to passengers, it was linked to the GN&GE line by a new south to west curve allowing trains to run direct from March to Dogsthorpe. Inward flows of freight were small but outward flows were initially quite large. The Dogsthorpe line was maintained primarily for brick traffic but the other routes dealt mainly with an outward flow of agricultural produce from the Fens. This outward flow of fruit, flowers and vegetables from the local market gardens and farms specialising in horticulture had also been a very important element in the freight traffic of the western section when the M&GN was fully operational. In the final years the Spalding to Sutton Bridge section was particularly busy. For example, in the first half of the 1960s Long Sutton still had an extensive outward flow of agricultural products to the London area, the Midlands and to the north. The goods were despatched in a parcels train at 4.45 pm and a freight at 5.15 pm. In addition to the highly perishable products such as flowers – up to 2,600 boxes a day could be loaded in season – the goods yard also despatched tinned products from a local canning factory. The end of these services began in 1964 and finally disappeared when the final freight spur in the west from Dogsthorpe to Murrow was closed in 1966.

Locomotive depots

During the 1950s most services on the M&GN lines were operated by engines based at one of four locomotive depots, Peterborough New England, South Lynn, Melton Constable and Yarmouth Beach. Each had their own allocation of engines, and the last three were concerned almost exclusively with working trains over the M&GN system. Prior to 1948, the M&GN also shared other railway's sheds at Bourne, Spalding and Peterborough. At the latter, it used the Midland Spital shed (named after the adjacent Spital Bridge) until the LNER takeover in 1936, after which the M&GN line locomotives transferred to the former Great Eastern Railway shed at Peterborough East. Then, in 1939, they moved again to the nearby New England shed which had been built by the Great Northern Railway.

During the BR era, the three purely M&GN sheds received the following shed codes – South Lynn 31D, Melton Constable 32G and Yarmouth Beach 32F. The code of a locomotive's 'home' shed was shown on a small oval plate fixed to the smokebox door.

After South Lynn was shed was closed it remained standing for many years, certainly into the mid-1980s, and it was eventually demolished to make way for a travellers' site. Similarly, a small diesel shunter was sometimes to be seen in the shed building at Melton Constable after the main closure, right until the passenger services ceased in 1964. The shed building here is still standing, although hemmed in and partially hidden by additions which have accumulated over the last 45 years. There was no after-life for Yarmouth shed – it had been allowed to deteriorate and was demolished in 1959. The metal work from the former Norwich City depot, which had been erected in 1942 after the original was destroyed in a German 'Baedeker' air raid, now forms part of the North Norfolk Railway's locomotive works at Weybourne.

COLOUR-RAIL

South Lynn shed was being modernised as the M&GN passenger services were being withdrawn. That such a newly rebuilt shed should be shut was considered absurd when its facilities were superior to those at the nearby ex-GER King's Lynn shed. Consequently South Lynn remained open until the end of steam in the area as a stabling and repair shed. Here ex-GER D16/2 class 62613 of March depot resides at South Lynn on 9 August 1960, three months before its withdrawal.

The M&GN Society's third fund raising rail tour on 27 May 1961 consisted of former Melton Constable-based 43151, by now a Peterborough New England engine, hauling a nine-coach train over the remnants of the M&GN lines in the Fens. Starting and finishing at Peterborough North it ran *via* the GER to March, and GE&GN Joint to Murrow where it joined the M&GN on the newly built spur. 43151 reversed into Murrow East, where it ran round the train and proceeded to Wisbech North, before returning to rejoin the GE&GN Joint for a run up to Spalding. Here it took the M&GN route to Sutton Bridge where it reversed again and went back to Spalding and this time took the M&GN to Bourne, reversed and headed back to Spalding for a final sprint back down the GNR line to Peterborough North. The train is seen here at Wisbech North, the then end of the line from Murrow. The engine has run around the train and is being prepared for the trip back to Murrow. Given the immaculate state of the station and track it is difficult to believe it had been closed for two years and that this was certainly the last passenger train to ever call here. The line closed completely in December 1964.

M&GN Specials

The M&GNJRS was formed by a group of enthusiasts on one of the last trains on 28 February 1959 with the intention of preserving the whole of the M&GN – a bold ambition in those days. They immediately set about raising funds to purchase all, or some, of the M&GN. Their ambition was achieved in 1965 when they succeeded in purchasing the line from Sheringham to Weybourne which was to become the North Norfolk Railway.

A good source of revenue in those early days was the running of enthusiast rail tours. In East Anglia many former passenger lines or sections of line remained open for goods traffic. Organising passenger trips over these lines was popular, and often complex itineraries were planned to cover as much remaining route as possible. Early trips included Norwich City to Norwich Thorpe *via* Melton Constable, Cromer, Tivetshall and Beccles, and stubs of the M&GN around the Fens. By the late 1960s the number of these freight lines was dwindling and more family orientated rail tours to far flung destinations across the UK developed under the M&GN Society banner which lasted until the early 1980s.

One branch on which freight trains continued to operate following withdrawal of passenger services was that between Norwich City and Melton Constable. This is the signalman's view of Norwich City station on Saturday 10 September 1960. The corrugated iron locomotive shed is on the left, and just beyond it WD 'Austerity' class 2-8-0 90709 is standing next to the water tower. Under BR, up to 1959, the locomotive depot was classified as a sub-shed of Melton Constable. In the centre of the photograph are the platforms of the now closed passenger station, whilst there is still plenty of activity in the goods yard to the right. The engine was allocated to March shed and had six more years to go before withdrawal.

Looking northwards from the signal box, the volume of goods traffic is even more noticeable, as 90709 runs forward to take over the 11.11 am goods for Norwich Thorpe. This was to be the very last working *via* Melton Constable and Sheringham, as the Themelthorpe connecting line was brought into use on the following Monday.

'Round the world' freight

After passenger services were withdrawn, several sections of the M&GN were retained for a few years to handle freight traffic. One of these was the branch line from Melton Constable to Norwich City, where there was a busy goods yard. This line also handled large quantities of concrete materials originating from a works at Lenwade.

However, with the total closure of the line westwards from Melton Constable, trains between Norwich City and the main line system were faced with a circuitous journey of over 60 miles by way of Melton Constable, Sheringham and North Walsham to Norwich Thorpe. The two Norwich stations were no more than three miles apart as the crow flies, and the trains following this route soon gained the nickname of 'round the world' freights. The volume of traffic was sufficient to justify the construction of a new connecting line at Themelthorpe, where the M&GN line passed over the old Great Eastern branch line from County School to Wroxham. As a result, the journey between the Norwich stations was reduced by some 20 miles after the new line opened on 12 September 1960.

A HARRISON/RJA COLLECTION

Most of the 'round the world' freight trains had no reason to call at Cromer Beach, so they took the avoiding line between Runton West and Newstead Lane Junctions. The remains of this long-forgotten line can still be seen today, on the left hand side of Bittern Line trains from Norwich as they descend eastwards into Cromer. 90709, as it heads for Norwich Thorpe, is coming off the cut-off line at Newstead Lane Junction to join the line from Cromer Beach to Norwich, which is to the left of the train. The first few wagons of the train are carrying concrete beams from the works at Lenwade, while the vans had come round from Norwich City.

Seen from the brake van, the empty wagons for one of the sand trains passes through Lenwade station on 14 April 1969, some ten years after the closure of the line to passengers. Superficially, very little had changed in that decade. The station was still fully signalled, with the signalman controlling the level crossing gates by a wheel inside the box. The photographer was travelling on the brake van as one of a party with a privately organised permit – it was amazing what you could achieve, if you asked, in those days!

The end of freight – Norwich branch

Goods trains continued to run by way of the Themelthorpe connecting line from Norwich Thorpe as far as Norwich City until 1969, by which time general goods traffic had faded away. The line between Norwich City and Drayton was closed that year, but Drayton yard remained in use for a regular traffic flow in locally quarried sand, bound for south London. This sand traffic had ceased by the early 1970s and the line was cut back to the concrete works at Lenwade in 1973.

With a general decline in use, the line between Lenwade and Themelthorpe was closed in 1982, some 23 years after it had lost its passenger trains.

A month earlier, on 14 March 1969, D5543 was photographed in the goods yard at Drayton. The locomotive has arrived with the empty sand wagons and deposited them in the Down platform, while it picks up the loaded wagons from the sidings. It propelled these into the vacant Up platform, then coupled on to the empties and shunted them into the yard, before running round the loaded train ready for departure. The diesel became 31125 and was withdrawn in December 1994.

D5579 stands in Drayton goods yard, having backed the empty wagons into the sidings on 14 April 1969. These will be left here for loading, to be collected later in the week. Although by then the yard was used only for the sand traffic, it still had a traditional appearance with the solid looking goods sheds and coal merchants still active in the area. The lines at Drayton were lifted in 1973, and an industrial estate now covers the site. As 31400, the locomotive was withdrawn in July 1991 and cut up two years later.

D5579 passes the platform at Lenwade with the loaded sand train on its way back from Drayton, again on 14 April 1969. The station building would survive into the 21st century, and the route of the railway was to become part of a long distance footpath, fittingly named 'Marriott's Way' to commemorate William Marriott's long and illustrious career on the M&GN. He was the driving force behind the railway between 1893 and 1924. The LMS 12-ton box van in the bay road remained there until after the track was lifted early in 1984 and was eventually cut up on site.

The only part of the M&GN that was kept open for passengers after the 1959 closure was Cromer to Melton Constable. This section became a victim of the infamous Dr Beeching whose axe subsequently truncated the line at Sheringham. Through trains from Norwich operated until 6 April 1964, and freight lasted a little longer until 28 December 1964. Here, on 7 March 1964, a signal stands sentinel on the approach to an empty Melton Constable from the former Norwich line. This line had been closed with the opening of the Themelthorpe curve.

This is a typical M&GN concrete post signal manufactured at Melton. The lying-on-its-side 'T' arm is for advising the driver that he is going into an occupied platform or that the line is occupied within the clearing point of West box Home at the other end of the station. The slang name for this distinctive warning signal was 'the hammer'. When the 'T' signal was cleared for a train to proceed, the enginemen and the signalmen referred to this as 'going in under the hammer'.

Within a year much of the railway infrastructure at Melton would be swept away forever. Only the old Works building, the 1950s engine shed and the original goods shed survive today in industrial use.

COLOUR-RAIL